MW01125265

Blind Taste Cultural Guidebooks # 1:

<u>Beyond Time</u>

Sampling & Savoring
in Caral & Supe, Peru

by Marco Bixecker and Luis Deza Leon

Publicaciones Aula Mundi

"Happiness is the road ..."

Bob Dylan, American songwriter,
'Chronicles, Vol. 1'

'Summary ...'

*"Wayra muyuyllam
muyuykamuchkani;
sambuchallaykiqa,
nigruchallaykiqa ..." ***

Traditional Quechua Chant

* *"I am coming, just like the visit of the wind;
your beloved, your beloved ..."*

The ancient city of Caral seems to whisper ancient songs like this traditional chant in Quechua, the indigenous language which has been spoken throughout Peru for centuries. But the English translation doesn't even come close to the intangible poetry which can be felt in the seemingly timeless and ageless ruins standing in the middle of the Peruvian desert, about 120 miles north of the capital, Lima. Modern reason struggles with the comprehension of such deep and profound impressions and mysteries. One has to resort to philosophers like Emmanuel Kant, who talked about "metaphysics" as "an inevitable necessity", or Arthur Schopenhauer, who defined the human being as a "metaphysical animal." Metaphysics and spirituality have certainly contributed to taking mankind beyond the simple search and use of fire as an instrument of power.

And both these cultural practices were key to a society which once built and occupied the ancient city of Caral. The inhabitants of this place may have spoken an early form of Quechua, the very language which the famous Incas spread across and beyond the Andes. Recent research seems to suggest that this old indigenous language might have originated in the coastal region of central Peru. Quechua is still being spoken in Peru and in neighboring countries in South America today. It has even found its way into Peruvian Spanish, where the word for "corn" is "choclo", derived from the Quechua word "chuqllu", for example. But language is not the only link between the past and the present. Food and culinary traditions in Peru are directly derived from ancient indigenous traditions and have been blended with the colonial cuisine of the Spanish Conquerors and with the restrictions and needs of the Republican era, shortly after independence, when people had to improvise and "invent" dishes with little means. And this culinary blend can be found near the main square, or "Plaza de Armas", in a small town officially known as "Supe Pueblo". A covered market reveals a delightful mosaic of colors, smells and tastes which symbolize the diversity of the culinary history of Peru. Supe itself is located at the crossroads between the Pan – American Highway, known as "La Panamericana Norte" in this region, and a dusty gravel road which follows the Supe River Valley towards the ancient city of Caral.

Most travelers tend to ignore Supe. But it is a convenient overnight base to explore the nearby archaeological and cultural treasures. This small town is a little gem with rough edges and provides an insight into authentic Peruvian life. Some of its streets might feel scary and neglected, and some of the people might look like shady characters, but it is the welcoming warmth and the genuine curiosity of the inhabitants that will overwhelm any open – minded traveler with a willingness to share and learn some words in Spanish. Spending a morning, an afternoon, or maybe a whole day or more in Supe is a grassroots experience with a down – to – earth vibe.

In comparison, it is hard to ignore the deep and profound energy which emanates from the ancient ruins of Caral. Reason and logic are constantly challenged and defied here. It is definitely recommendable to explore the old city with a guide. Some of the guides at the archaeological site speak enough English to share some basic information, data and facts about the culture that once thrived here. But the ability to speak some Spanish would allow a traveler to find out how people refer to these monuments and their significance personally, in our day and age.

Maybe the most important way to connect with the ancient city in the desert is silence. And silence speaks many languages.

One might then be able to feel that there is something strange and unspeakable about this place. And yet, it is not an unpleasant experience. Obviously, modern education warns us against intangible impressions like this. Maybe that's the reason why many people are afraid of the mysteries of the past. Even the word "Caral" has lost its tangible significance.

Modern linguists and scholars still keep arguing about the real meaning of that word. But the sound of it conjures up images of seafood, fresh vegetables and delicious fruit shared around a bonfire at the foot of a large pyramid in the middle of the coastal desert. One can hear laughter, music and ancient voices echoing, singing and speaking through the ages.

Caral means continuity through space and beyond time …

'Situations & Snapshots ...'

"It is not down in any map;
true places never are ..."

Herman Melville, American writer,
'Moby Dick'

"the archaeological site of Caral ..."

Y *'Breakfast in Supe ...'*

The small town of Supe is located 2 hours north of Lima, near the turnoff to Caral. The archaeological site of Caral is located 20 miles from Supe. But the 'Plaza de Armas', the main square in Supe, should be your first destination if you are looking for a real breakfast.

A small cafe known as 'Restaurant – Fuente de Soda Enma' is frequented by many locals. And you could sit down among them, at a sidewalk table, and order some 'cafe pasado', 'filtered coffee', and two egg sandwiches, for example.

On the main plaza you will also find the 'Museo Comunitario'. It is an interpretive center for the ancient city located in the nearby desert.

Y *"the 'Museo Comunitario' in Supe ..."*

'Locals and Protagonists ...'

The town hall of Supe is also located on the main plaza.
If you got the chance to speak with Juan Carlos Albújar Pereyra, the mayor of Supe at the time this is being written, he would proudly highlight some of the culinary treasures of this region.
The archaeologist responsible for the scientific study of the ancient city of Caral is a woman by the name of Ruth Shady Solís. She and her team determined the age of the ruins and concluded that it is probably the oldest city in South America. It was built around 2,600 B.C., a discovery that has raised more questions than it has answered.
One of the guides at the archaeological site of Caral, Dino Augurto, would be more than happy to share some of his knowledge about Caral with you. He originally comes from the Piura region in northern Peru. And he tends to match his cultural background with the ancient traditions of the Supe River Valley some of which date back to the old civilization of Caral.
Then there is a real local character known as 'Chapi'.
Everybody knows her by her nickname and she is always eager to chat with people at her stall in the covered market in Supe.
Finally you might even be able to meet Coral Herencia occasionally.
Even though she lives and works in Lima she admires the ancient ruins of Caral which she visits as often as she can and with which she connects in a spiritual way as a so – called 'chamana' or 'shaman'.
One might say that she is an indigenous Peruvian priestess who conveys the timeless message of her ancestors.

'Lunch in Supe ...'

A detour to a small traditional restaurant by the name of 'El Acuario', which is located at the outskirts of Supe, is definitely worth the time. But make sure that it is open. Ask for a traditional dish, known as 'Papa A La Huancaína'. It should be the first course. It consists of potatoes served with a creamy sauce, some hard boiled eggs and some lettuce. It should be followed by 'Ceviche De Pollo', 'Chicken Ceviche', a delicious and spicy specialty from northern Peru. You will find out that everything is very delicious largely thanks to an ancestral tradition which consists of mixing all kinds of natural herbs and spices to give dishes like that some flavor.

And then there is the inevitable 'ají' sauce, a typical Peruvian sauce made with hot peppers, which pretty much accompanies every major meal.

"'Papa A La Huancaína' ..."

'Caral ...'

Now, why is the ancient city of Caral so important ?
First, there is its age that has been scientifically established by Ruth Shady Solís and her team. The oldest ruins are approximately 5,000 years old which means that this city already thrived while the pyramids of Egypt were still being built.
And apparently it was inhabited by a peaceful society since no evidence of warfare has been uncovered yet, and this would make Caral quite unique in world history and anthropology. Some indications suggest that Caral and the surrounding Supe River Valley were a fertile agricultural region with trade routes and networks reaching as far as the Amazon.

"why is the ancient city of Caral
so important ?"

'Caral in the late afternoon ...'

It would definitely be a privilege to arrive at the ancient city of Caral in the late afternoon. The fading daylight has an intensity which reaches epic proportions due to the pyramids, buildings, temples and shrines that are spread across a dusty plain close to the fertile Supe River Valley with the barren foothills and higher mountains of the Andes in the background. The archaeological site emanates a sense of magic and majesty with its sweeping vistas and open views. The air is so clear and dry that it muffles the sounds of your footsteps, the noises of human chatter and the clicking of cameras.

"the ancient city of Caral
in the late afternoon ..."

"[the] archaeological site emanates
a sense of magic and majesty ..."

'The 'Pago A La Tierra ...'

Usually, in late October or early November, the ceremony of the 'Pago A La Tierra' is held in the ancient city. Guides and other staff will be busy rounding up visitors and lighting torches as the dusk slowly fades into the night. You are about to witness an ancient form of Thanksgiving.

It will be a colorful ceremony with the presence of some ancient musical instruments as they were known to the inhabitants of Caral and to the famous Inca Lords thousands of years later.

A spiritual leader will conduct the whole ceremony. He or she is usually referred to as the 'maestro' or 'maestra', in other words, the 'leader of the ritual'.

It is the leader's role to perform several songs, to recite some ancient prayers and some traditional poetry, to give thanks to the 'Earth Mother' and to invite everyone to make a little gift to 'our Mother', the Earth, so that She may protect and bless the audience with the ancient crops that the inhabitants of this place grew and harvested. The team of Ruth Shady Solís has found evidence which suggests that music was quite important at Caral. Flutes and other so – called primitive instruments have been uncovered and some of the music that is played during the ceremony of the 'Pago A La Tierra' is performed on replicas of those ancient instruments.

"the 'Pago A La Tierra' ..."

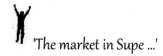

'Spending the night in Supe ...'

If you decide to spend a night in this area rather than going back to Lima, the funny receptionist at the 'Hotel Turístico Rinconcito Supano' will be a delight to chat with for a couple of minutes.

The hotel itself is conveniently located on the main plaza in Supe.

The next morning you might agree with the assumption that there is nothing like coffee to get you going. And, if a delicious snack like a 'Tamal Supano' comes with it, it is even better. And this is just one of the many local delicacies on the menu at the hotel – restaurant downstairs.

'The market in Supe ...'

Then a stroll to the nearby covered market will allow you to notice that many of the vendors are as interesting and colorful as the produce which they sell. Make sure to stop and chat with some of them. For example, there is a small delightful woman whom everybody knows by her nickname, Chapi.

The local delicacy which she sells is called 'picarones de yuca'. The closest full English translation for this sweet snack would be 'cassava fritters' or 'manioc fritters'. And in a short conversation Chapi might even give you her recipe for a Peruvian delight which is hardly known outside the Spanish – speaking world.

'The 'Norte Chico' Civilization ...'

In the late morning or by noon you might want to go back to the ruins of Caral and experience them at broad daylight. Again, this is a desert, the large and seemingly endless coastal desert of Peru. But it is an area which was once the homeland of one of the earliest civilizations in the Americas. The ancient city of Caral and the surrounding Supe River Valley were the center of the so – called 'Norte Chico' culture named after the arid region located north of Lima and south of Trujillo, in northern Peru.

The 'Norte Chico' Civilization is still shrouded in mystery. It is often described as a 'pre – ceramic' society which excelled in architecture as the pyramids and temples at Caral clearly demonstrate.

Maybe you are going to run into Dino Augurto while he is busy explaining to a group of visitors how the anti – seismic building methods, which the ancient inhabitants of this city used, allowed them to build all these imposing pyramids and temples thousands of years before the Incas erected their own monuments and shrines. Some people even think that the latter adopted the building techniques of the 'Norte Chico' Civilization and of other cultural groups in ancient Peru.

"the large and seemingly endless
coastal desert of Peru ..."

"agriculture allowed the
'Norte Chico' Civilization to thrive for centuries ..."

"pyramids and temples ..."

'Lunch at Caral ...'

If you happen to be here during the weekend when the ceremony of the 'Pago A La Tierra' is held you might be able to enjoy a traditional lunch at the headquarters of the archaeological site the day after the ritual.

The meal is composed of pre – Columbian, indigenous and traditional Peruvian dishes and drinks such as 'chicha de guayaba', a slightly fermented juice made from the guava plant. Based on archaeological evidence and recent findings scholars have concluded that seafood and the early stages of food production based on agriculture allowed the 'Norte Chico' Civilization to thrive for centuries. Adjusted to the modern notion of gourmet eating, you would be able to enjoy an almost poetic symphony of tastes, colors, smells and sensations.

" an almost poetic symphony
of tastes, colors, smells and sensations ..."

'Ruth Shady Solís ...'

That same weekend you might even get the chance to meet Ruth Shady Solís herself. Maybe she is going to give a press conference at the headquarters of Caral.

"Doctora', what can today's society learn from a culture that existed 5,000 years ago ?' "Doctora', how has your cultural identity as a Peruvian changed since the discovery of Caral ?'

If you asked her questions like that and listened to her answers you would come to the conclusion that the ancient inhabitants of Caral would be proud of what Doctor Ruth Shady Solís has accomplished.

"What can today's society learn
from a culture that existed
5,000 years ago ? ..."

Y 'The 'Maestra' ...'

If you are lucky enough you might be able to chat with a spiritual person like Coral Herencia, one of the ceremonial leaders of the 'Pago A La Tierra'. She might even introduce herself in Quechua.
And you might notice that her words and statements are so profound that they don't seem to come from her mouth but directly from her heart and soul, and even from the heart and soul of her indigenous ancestors and forefathers. She might also stress the spiritual significance of the ancient city of Caral. Interestingly enough, her thought – provoking comments would correspond to the scientific theories about this site. Based on recent findings and research, scholars have concluded that Caral was a religious center as well as an urban center which would make the word 'city – state' adequate enough to describe this place in the middle of the desert.

Y *"Caral was a religious center ..."*

'Sites & Sensations ...'

*"...la cuisine d'une société est un langage dans lequel elle traduit inconsciemment sa structure ..." ***

*Claude Levi-Strauss,
French anthropologist*

* *"cooking is a language into which a society unconsciously translates its structure ..."*

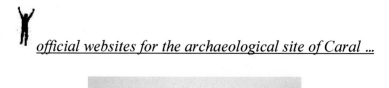

official websites for the archaeological site of Caral ...

... www.caralperu.gob.pe

... www.zonacaral.gob.pe

official website for the small town of Supe
(Supe Pueblo) ...

... www.munisupe.gob.pe

'Restaurant - Fuente de Soda Enma' ...

… offers 'café pasado' (filtered coffee) and breakfast sandwiches
on the main plaza in Supe

Location: Plaza de Armas, Supe

 *'Chef's Recommendation for'* ...

… '1 Breakfast Egg Sandwich':

"2 scrambled eggs, salt and pepper for seasoning,
2 tablespoons of Greek yoghurt,
4 slices of country bread, 1 slice of ham,
4 slices of tomato.

Scramble the eggs and season with salt and pepper.
Add the yoghurt.
Spread on a slice of bread. Put the ham and
2 slices of tomato on another slice of bread.
Then press down ..."

'Chef's Recommendation for' ...

… 'Papa A La Huancaína':

Location: 'El Acuario', Urb. San Nicolas, Supe, Peru

"This dish originally comes from the Peruvian Andes,
and more specifically from the department of Huancayo
located in the central Andean region·
It is an area known for its dairy products·
The creamy sauce for this dish is made by blending milk,
cheese, soaked bread and 'ají amarillo',
a Peruvian yellow hot chilli pepper·
It is poured over some sliced Andean potatoes
and served with boiled eggs and with olives ..."

'Chef's Recommendation for' ...

… 'Ceviche de Pollo Al Estilo Norteño':
('Northern Style Chicken Ceviche')

"It is composed of several pieces of fried chicken marinated in onions and yellow hot chili peppers· It is not to be confused with seafood ceviche ..."

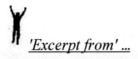 *'Excerpt from'* ...

… the greetings in Quechua during the opening ceremony of the
'Pago A La Tierra' at the ancient city of Caral

"Allinllanchu, taytaykuna, mamaykuna ..." *

(Coral Herencia, ceremonial leader)

* *"Welcome, ladies and gentlemen ..."*

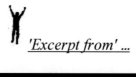

'Excerpt from' ...

… a chant and prayer during the ceremony of the
'Pago A La Tierra' at the ancient city of Caral

"Thank you, Lord (of Caral),
thank you for your teachings ..."

(Coral Herencia, ceremonial leader)

'Excerpt from' ...

… a chant and prayer during the closing ceremony of the
'Pago A La Tierra' at the ancient city of Caral

"We are offering our best crops,
We are offering our hearts,
Let's share happiness and reciprocity,
Let's remember how to weave the net,
How to build a community ..."

(Coral Herencia, ceremonial leader)

'Hotel Caral Supe' ...

… is a decent place to stay
in the center of the small town of Supe

Location:
Esqu. Gr. San Martin 515
con Gr. Bolognesi 504 – Plaza de Armas

Email: administracion@hotelcaralsupe.com
Website: www.hotelcaralsupe.com

'Hotel Turístico Rinconcito Supano' ...

… is another, slightly fancier and more expensive, option on the outskirts of town

Website: www.rinconcitosupano.com
Facebook: 'Rinoncito Supano'

'Chef's Recommendation for' ...

... 'Picarones de Yuca', which 'Chapi' sells
at the market in Supe

Location:
Mercado n° 1 Supe Pueblo

'Picarones de Yuca …'
('Cassava Fritters' or 'Manioc Fritters …')

"First you have to roll the 'yucca'
(manioc or cassava), like dough·
Then you add cinnamon, anise, clove,
and as much sugar as you like·
And this is how you make the dough·
Then you wrap it up· You can fry it·
But you could also parboil it or steam it …"

('Chapi', market vendor)

'Chef's Recommendation for' ...

… 'Tamales Supanos' available at Tamales 'Marengo's'
Eduardo Raul Alarcon Cavero y Sra.

Location: Mercado n° 1 Supe Pueblo

Email.: tamales_marengos@hotmail.com
Website: www.facebook.com/tamalesdesupemarengos

'Tamales Supanos ...'

"*This specialty is made of ground corn which is mixed
with 'ají', chicken or pork meat, and ...
It has a specific reddish color due to the paprika
which we put in the 'ají' sauce·
We also add a little bit of anise and some peanuts
to give it a distinct flavor·
And this dough is wrapped in banana leaves·
This is what we call a 'tamal' ('tamale')·
Then we boil it for two or three hours ...*"

(Juan Carlos Albújar Pereyra, mayor of Supe)

'Excerpt from' ...

… a dance performance at Áspero, another archaeological site
located in the coastal part of the Caral / Supe region;
the music is performed with replicas of the ancient bone flutes
which had been discovered at the archaeological site of Caral,
while the lyrics are meant to reflect the ancient connection between
the Pacific Coast, the Andes and the Amazon

"I am Machín, the white monkey from Marañón,
I am the wise little monkey that makes everyone laugh,
When the jaguar is roaring ...

The little monkey sneaks up behind him and pulls his tail,
'Do not devour me, 'Tío Tigre'', says Machín,
'Or else I am going to tell the little ants
to bite you in the belly,
And the little bees will sting you in the ears ...'

So, the wise little monkey makes the jaguar run away,
The funny little monkey scares him
and makes him run away ..."

('Mono Machín',
a traditional song from the Peruvian Amazon region,
Juan Luis Dammert & Grupo CEMDUC)

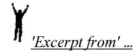 *'Excerpt from'* ...

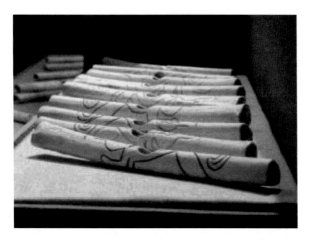

... a lecture on how to play a traditional melody on the replica of an ancient bone flute discovered at the archaeological site of Caral

"Please, keep in mind
that the face of the monkey
has to be on the right – hand side
when you're holding the flute ..."

('Maestro Carlos', teacher and performer)

'Excerpt from' ...

… a South American folk song
inspired by the ancient city of Caral

"stone, mud and sweat;
[...] flutes expressing love;
city without wars,
empire of happiness,
in the moonlight from the Andes to the Sea ..."

(Mauricio Venegas – Astorga, Chilean songwriter)

'Chef's Recommendation for' ...

… 'Pepián de Choclo con Anchovetas Arrebosadas':
('Corn Chili Stew with Coated Anchovies')

"This is a dish from northern Peru.
It is composed of tender ground corn mixed with
'ají colorado' ('sun dried red hot chili peppers') or
'ají mirasol' ('sun dried yellow hot chili peppers').
The stew can be made with pieces of pork,
chicken or beef. But in this specific case
it comes with anchovies coated with eggs and flour ..."

… 'Chicha de Guayaba'
('Guava Chicha')

"We have concluded that the ancient people of Caral probably made and consumed 'chicha de guayaba', a guava beer, or fermented guava chicha, during ceremonies and major events ..."

(Dino Augurto, interpretive guide at the archaeological site of Caral)

'Chef's Recommendation for' ...

… 'Causa Rellena Con Anchovetas':
('Causa Stuffed With Anchovies')

... 'Causa Rellena Con Anchovetas':
('Causa Stuffed With Anchovies')

"Legend has it that this dish was 'invented' during the
'War of the Pacific', between Peru and Chile,
which lasted from 1879 to 1883.
Due to the lack of resources, cooks and chefs had to
invent recipes with the few ingredients they had.
One of them comes down to blending and mashing
potatoes and fish. Often the author of such a makeshift
meal would say, 'por la causa', 'for the cause'.
Supposedly this is where the name of this dish,
'Causa', comes from. It is composed of mashed potatoes
mixed with yellow hot chili peppers and lime juice.
Depending on the region and on the available resources
other ingredients might be added such as
lettuce, spinach, eggs, or, as in this case,
anchovies, boiled eggs and olives ..."

'Chef's Recommendation for' ...

… 'Mazamorra de Calabaza':
('Pumpkin Pudding' or 'Squash Pudding')

… 'Mazamorra de Calabaza':
('Pumpkin Pudding' or 'Squash Pudding')

Ingredients:
1 ripe squash or pumpkin, 1 cup of water (or milk),
1 slice of cinnamon, 4 cloves,
½ teaspoon or 4 pinches of dark brown sugar,
1 cup of brown sugar, maybe a couple of raisins …

Preparation:
slice and peel the squash or pumpkin, then cut it up into
small pieces; boil it, adding the water (or milk), the
cinnamon, the cloves and the dark brown sugar;
stir constantly;
add the brown sugar when it is boiled
and stir thoroughly …

Special Advice:
for this typical dessert from northern Peru it is best to
use a squash or pumpkin with a yellow color
and with black seeds …"

Luis Deza León ...

… is a freelance journalist and Peruvian chef.
He can organize trips and excursions to Caral and the surrounding area from Lima, his hometown. He is a professional driver with a long experience as a guide,
and he is very knowledgeable about local history.

Email.:   dezaleonluis@hotmail.com

"When I first visited the ancient city of Caral, I experienced a magical encounter with our surprising history· I marveled at the great civilization which we Peruvians come from· We should learn from the social organization of our ancestors to solve the problems that still afflict our society today ..."

'Sketches & Statistics ...'

*"I completed a map of the countrey ** which we have been passing ..."*

William Clark, American explorer, 'The Journals of Lewis & Clark'

*** original misspelling for 'country' in the 'Journals of Lewis & Clark'*

<u>~ 9,210 B.C.:</u>
earliest indication of human settlement
at the central Peruvian coast,
near Caral and the Supe River Valley ...

<u>~ 3,000 B.C. to ~ 1,800 B.C.:</u>
during the so – called 'Pre – Ceramic Period',
or 'Late Archaic Period', the 'Norte Chico' Civilization,
also known as the 'Caral' Civilization,
flourishes around the ancient city of Caral,
located in the Supe River Valley,
apparently without the development of full scale agriculture,
craft specialization, a writing system, ceramic production,
social stratification, or metallurgy ...

<u>~ 1,800 B.C. to ~ 1,500 B.C.:</u>
ceramics and pottery begin to appear at the Peruvian coast
launching the so – called 'Initial Period',
while the ancient city of Caral loses prestige ...

<u>~ 1,000 B.C.:</u>
after having been abandoned for centuries,
Caral is briefly occupied during the so – called
'Middle Formative Period', or 'Early Horizon Period' ...

<u>~ 900 A.D. to ~ 1,400 A.D.:</u>
another settlement on the outskirts of the ancient city
has no impact on the monuments during the so – called
'States Period' or 'Lordships Period' ...

<u>16th century:</u>
the Spanish chronicler Pedro Cieza de León claims that
Quechua (the predominant language of the Inca Civilization)
originated at the Peruvian coast ...

<u>1905:</u>
Caral is 'rediscovered',
but the idea of exploring the city is quickly abandoned ...

<u>1948 – 1949:</u>
the American historian Paul Kosok conducts extensive
field studies of several ancient irrigation systems
in the oasis valleys of the coastal desert in Peru,
including in the Supe River Valley ...

1974:
the American anthropologist Michael E. Moseley publishes
an article in which he claims that Andean Civilization
originated at the Pacific Coast of Peru ...

1978:
Ruth Shady Solís hears about Caral for the first time,
while visiting the so - called 'Chupacigarro Hacienda',
in the Supe River Valley ...

1979:
the French archaeologist Frederic Engel
visits the site also known as 'Chupacigarro Grande'
(the site referred to as 'Caral' nowadays);
in his book 'De Las Begonias Al Maíz'
('From Begonias to Corn'), first published in 1987,
he claims that some of the pyramids and ruins
he saw must have been built prior to the appearance
of pottery and ceramics in the Peruvian Andes ...

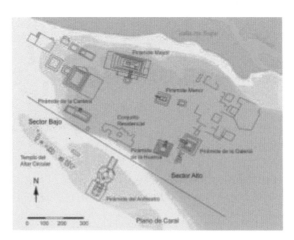

<u>1994:</u>
Peruvian archaeologists, led by Ruth Shady Solís,
start conducting scientific research at Caral ...

<u>1997:</u>
Ruth Shady Solís suggests for the first time that Caral
might be the oldest city on the American continent ...

<u>2001:</u>
the April 27 issue of the international journal Science
reveals scientific evidence confirming that Caral is
the oldest urban center in the Americas ...

<u>2002:</u>
the Peruvian linguist and anthropologist
Alfredo Torero publishes his final work,
'Idiomas de los Andes, Lingüística e Historia'
('Languages of the Andes, Linguistics and History');
throughout his scientific career he has tried to prove
the coastal origin of the Quechua language by doing research
in places like the Supe River Valley ...

2002:
the BBC publishes a documentary entitled
'The Lost Pyramids of Caral',
in which the archaeological site is presented as a
'mother – city' for the ancient cultures of Peru ...

2003:
the Peruvian government launches the
'Proyecto Especial Arqueológico Caral – Supe'
('Special Archaeological Project Caral – Supe')
led by Ruth Shady Solís ...

2004:
the American archaeologists Jonathan Haas
and Winifred Creamer publish an article
in the magazine *Nature* describing
fieldwork and radiocarbon dating at Caral ...

2009:
the ancient city of Caral is declared
a world heritage site by UNESCO ...

2010:
the 'Proyecto Especial Arqueológico Caral – Supe'
('Special Archaeological Project Caral – Supe') is renamed
'Zona Arqueológica Caral' ('Archaeological Area of Caral');
it includes 10 archaeological sites in the Supe River Valley ...

Today:
many unsettled questions about the 'Norte Chico Civilization'
and Caral remain unanswered while research continues ...

'2,627':
year 'Before Christ' ('B.C.'),
when Caral was in existence as evidenced
by radiocarbon dating conducted
by the Field Institute in Chicago ...

'30':
estimated total number of ancient major population centers
located in what is now the Norte Chico region,
north of Lima, Peru ...

'3000':
estimated minimal number of inhabitants
who once lived in Caral ...

'20,000':
possible total population in the entire Supe River Valley
thousands of years ago ...

'120':
distance in miles between Lima
and the archaeological site of Caral ...

'15':
distance in miles between Caral
and the Pacific Coast of northern Peru,
the main source of protein for the 'Norte Chico' Civilization ...

'18':
estimated total number of ancient urban centers
identified in the Supe River Valley ...

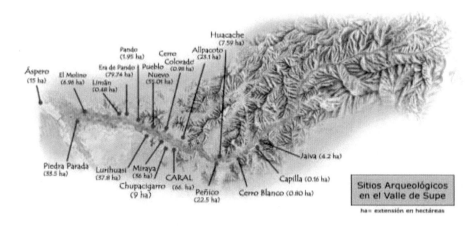

'32':
number of flutes made of condor and pelican bones
decorated with images of supernatural beings
uncovered at the archaeological site of Caral,
demonstrating the importance of music and religion
for the ancient inhabitants of the sacred city ...

'10° 53' 28.82" S & 77° 31' 04.32" W':
geographical coordinates of the ancient city of Caral ...

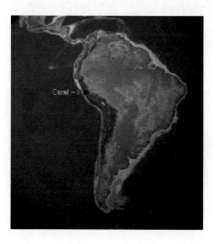

'Sounds & Symbols ...'

*"Le dictionnaire est
une machine à rêver." ***

Roland Barthes, French sociologist

* *"The dictionary is a dream machine."*

Caral [ka – 'RAL]   *"~ fiber (?); ~ reed (?)"*
"According to research conducted by Peruvian scholars and scientists, such as the linguist and anthropologist Alfredo Torero, the Quechua language might have originated at the Peruvian coast and maybe even in the 'Norte Chico' region (north of Lima) and in the Supe River Valley. Others insist that Quechua was born in the mountains of Bolivia. Linguistic studies realized by researchers at the prestigious University of San Marcos in Lima, Peru, show similarities between various place names in the 'Norte Chico' region and some Quechua words. They are often attributed to what is called 'Proto – Quechua', a prehistoric language which might have preceded the Quechua language predominantly spoken by the Incas. Even the French anthropologist Claude Levi – Strauss suggested that in many cultures all over the world ancient 'sacred words have lost their meaning, but might be used to name things and places'. As to the meaning of the name 'Caral' itself, some scholars believe that it means 'fiber' or 'reed' clearly demonstrating the importance of reeds in northern Peru. A 'modern' Quechua word for 'fiber' is 'pita'. The word 'reed' means 'matara' or 'totora' in the Quechua language. Even nowadays the so – called 'caballitos de totora' ('reed boats' or 'reed canoes') can be seen and are used by fishermen on Lake Titicaca, in the Andes, and on the Peruvian coast ..."

"Caral ..."

aji [a – 'HEE]:   **"chili pepper"**
"The pronunciation, [a – 'HEE], was imported by the Spanish Conquistadors to Peru from the indigenous Arawak people of the Caribbean. Since ancient times indigenous people throughout the Americas used various types of chili peppers to add more flavor to food items and meals that had a dull taste. The Quechua word for 'aji' is 'uchu'. Some of the varieties of 'aji' found in Peru include 'aji amarillo' ('yellow hot chili pepper'); 'aji colorado', a variety of 'aji' from the Peruvian Andes; 'aji mirasol' ('sun dried yellow hot chili pepper'); and 'aji panca' ('sun dried red hot pepper'), a variety mainly cultivated near the Peruvian coast ..."

algodón [al – go – 'DON]   **"cotton"**
"Cotton seeds were found all over the ancient city of Caral. Cotton was cultivated in the Supe River Valley and used to make fishing nets, textiles, bags and baskets. It would seem that the climate was more humid than it is today in northern Peru making the irrigation of large cotton fields possible. Thanks to the invention of cotton nets a fishing industry developed at nearby Áspero. Cotton textiles had different designs made with natural fibers and had both a domestic and a ritual function. The discovery of plant fibers at the archaeological site of Caral also indicates that reeds were woven into loose sacks, known as 'shicra bags'. They became an essential part in the process of building mounds, temples and pyramids at Caral since workers were able to fill those bags with rocks taken from a nearby quarry in the foothills of the Andes. Reed baskets could be used to store food items. Prior to the appearance of ceramics and pottery in South America people would use woven baskets as kitchen utensils eating directly out of their baskets, a practice which can still be observed among indigenous cultures nowadays. The Quechua word for 'cotton' is 'utkhu'. A 'cotton field' is referred to as 'utkhu chakra' ..."

anchovetas *[an – tcho – 'VE – tas]*   **"(Peruvian) anchovies"**
"Fishermen from nearby Áspero provided seafood and other fish for the inhabitants at Caral, including clams, mussels, anchovies and sardines, as the remains of seafood found at the archaeological site of Caral suggest. In Quechua 'choqe challwa' means 'anchovy'. 'Choqe' itself means 'gold', while 'challwa' means 'fish'. The words 'charki challwa' are used for 'dried fish'. There are indications which suggest that dried fish, and especially dried anchovies, were used as a form of currency. Nowadays anchovies are regarded as a 'minor' fish species by Western chefs and customers who only think of them as a garnish for pizza. But in ancient Peru they were considered what indigenous societies would call 'savior – fish' providing a large amount of protein for villages and cities like Caral, thus allowing an entire civilization to survive and prosper ..."

calabaza *[ka – la – 'BA – sa]*   **"pumpkin; squash; gourd"**
"Pumpkins, gourds and squash all belong to the same Cucurbita family. Native to the Americas, they were widely cultivated by American Indians before Europeans arrived. They are still cultivated extensively in the Andean highlands. Caral's inhabitants also grew crops such as beans, squash and cotton, building a network of irrigation canals in the Supe River Valley. In the Quechua language several words are used for 'calabaza', depending on the sub – species, the dialect and the region. The most common word is 'puru' or 'p'uru' ..."

chicha *['TCHEE – tcha]*   **"traditional beverage made from corn"**

"It is frequently fermented and still has a ritual function in Andean cultures. It is often translated as 'corn beer'. Spiritual purposes and religious festivals were key reasons to make, produce and consume this ancient drink. It is said to have medicinal qualities and is often used as an ingredient in traditional Peruvian cuisine. The most common Quechua word for 'chicha' is 'aqha' (or 'aqa') ..."

choclo *['TCHOK – lo]*   **"(Peruvian) corn; corncob"**

"The Peruvian Spanish word 'choclo' is derived from the Quechua word 'chuqllu' (or 'choqllo' or 'choqllu'), which also refers to 'cooked and tender corn on its cob', a widespread dish throughout the Andes. Corn is an inevitable side dish and key ingredient in Peruvian cuisine and can also be eaten as a sweet or salty snack ..."

Chupacigarro *[tshoo – pa – see – 'GA – ro]*   **"name of a bird species in the Supe River Valley"**

"In 1978 the Peruvian archaeologist Ruth Shady Solís was visiting the so – called 'Chupacigarro Hacienda' when she heard about Caral for the first time. 30 years earlier, in 1948, the American historian Paul Kosok, who later worked with Maria Reiche on the Nazca lines in southern Peru, studied a place in the Supe River Valley known as 'Chupacigarro Grande', thus named after a native bird species in the same region. This site would later be referred to as 'Caral'. Specifically, it consists of two circular sunken plazas that are the clearest indication that ceremonial activities took place in that area thousands of years ago. Large designs carved into the ground have also been discovered there. Those 'geoglyphs' would be given the name of the nearby hacienda, 'Chupacigarro'. They seem to demonstrate that similar designs and 'geoglyphs' found in the Nazca desert in southern Peru and in the Atacama desert in northern Chile might have been influenced by the 'Norte Chico Civilization' which flourished at Caral. So, the ancient city has clearly been a religious center and one of the first 'city – states' in the world which also suggests that political thinking was being developed on the Peruvian coast much earlier than scholars had believed. Caral itself would later be called a 'sacred city' by the Peruvian archaeologist Ruth Shady Solís in one of her books. In Quechua the word 'manqos' is used for a 'sacred site where ceremonies are held' ..."

"manqos ..."

flauta ['FLAOO – ta]   **"flute"**
"There is evidence that ceremonial feasts were held at Caral. During these rituals the inhabitants of the ancient city probably consumed alcohol and played music using flutes made of pelican and condor bones. Horns or cornets made from llama and alpaca bones have also been found at the archaeological site. The flutes which have been uncovered are decorated with carvings representing various animals, including monkeys and snakes which live in the Amazon region. This seems to indicate that there was an early network of trade routes across the Andes, between the Pacific Coast and the jungle. In aboriginal cultures the flute is often associated with 'magic', and the act of playing often has a ritual function. Musicians at Caral played small flutes. The Quechua word for 'small flute' is 'qena' or 'qina' from which the word 'quena' is derived ..."

guayaba [gwa – 'YA – va]   **"guava; guava plant; guava tree"**
"This tropical fruit has a strong, sweet aroma. It belongs to the group of edible plants which were domesticated at Caral and in the nearby Supe River Valley. Even nowadays it is used to brew 'guava chicha' or 'guava beer'. In Quechua the guava plant is referred to as 'sawintu' ..."

mazamorra [ma – sa – 'MO – ra]   **"porridge; pudding**
"Usually the word 'mazamorra' refers to a milky pudding made with corn, sugar and honey. But the word is also used for a squash pudding with ingredients like squash or pumpkin, milk and cinnamon. The Quechua word for 'mazamorra' is 'api' ..."

Norte Chico ['NOR – te 'TCHEE – ko]   *"a specific region in Peru, located north of Lima"*

"This region is located in coastal Peru, about 150 to 200 kilometers (90 to 150 miles) north of Lima. It is bounded by the Andes to the east, the Pacific Ocean to the west, the Lurín Valley to the south and the Casma Valley to the north. Four major river valleys cross this region from the Andes to the Pacific Ocean. One of them is the Supe River Valley which is where the ancient city of Caral is located. People in the Norte Chico region probably roasted their crops since pottery and ceramics for boiling and cooking had not yet appeared on the Peruvian Coast ..."

Pago A La Tierra ['PA – go a la 'TYE – ra]   *"Tribute to the Earth Mother"*

"In Quechua the act of paying tribute to the Earth Mother is referred to as 'pachamaman hayway'. Literally it means 'to offer food to Mother Earth'. The word 'Pachamama' (or 'Mamapacha') means 'Mother Earth' or 'Earth Mother'. It is composed of two other words. 'Pacha' means 'time', 'earth' and 'world', and it is often used in a spiritual way. The word 'mama' means 'mother' or 'lady'. On the other hand, the word 'hayway' means 'to invite', 'to share' and 'to offer food'. As part of the ceremony, the 'maestro' or 'maestra' (the 'priest' or 'priestess') sprinkles some 'chicha' as an offering to the 'spirits of the mountains' ('apus') and to the 'Earth Mother' ('Pachamama'). Ritual singing accompanies the ceremony. Songs are generally led by the 'maestro' or 'maestra' who becomes the 'leader' of the ceremony. Listeners might even hear ancient words which have lost their specific meaning over time. But they keep their spiritual significance in a ritual like the 'Pago A La Tierra' and survive in traditional songs.

In Latin American Spanish the word 'maestro' or 'maestra' means 'teacher'. It also refers to a religious leader, to a priest or priestess, and to a healer. The Quechua word 'aranwachiq' literally describes a 'leader of the ceremony'. For 'song' the word 'taki' is used in the Quechua language. More specifically it means 'chant'. Another Quechua word, 'wanka', refers to a ritual form of music dedicated to 'Mother Earth' ('Pachamama'). Generally speaking, on a worldwide scale and throughout history, the domestication of plants and crops coincided with mental and spiritual domestication contributing to rituals and ceremonies which often consisted of praying to the Gods for fertility. Indigenous cultures began to worship their food and associate many spirits, deities and gods with it. That way, the ancient inhabitants of Caral combined religious practices, ceremonies and rituals with their own crops and food staples ..."

"pachamaman hayway ..."

papa *['PA – pa]*   ***"potato"***

"The English word 'potato' is directly derived from the European Spanish word 'patata'. The Spaniards probably heard the most common original Quechua word for 'potato', 'papa', used as the direct object of a verb in which case the suffix '– ta' is added. So, the word 'papa' becomes 'papata'. Like so many other indigenous words, the Spanish Conquistadors probably adjusted 'papata' to their European pronunciation thus creating a new word, 'patata'. Depending on the region and the dialect, there are at least 30 words for 'potato' and its varieties in the Quechua language. Other than 'papa', which is the general word for 'potato', words like 'ulluku', 'araq', 'machka', 'yaku' and 'amachu' stand out. 'Ulluku' describes 'an edible Andean tuber'. 'Araq' is a Quechua word for 'wild potato'. Wild potatoes were an important food source for hunter – gatherers in the Americas long before the arrival of agriculture. The word 'machka' refers to a 'starchy potato'. 'Yaku' means 'juicy potato' in the Quechua language. Potatoes were also used for medicinal purposes. The Quechua word 'amachu' describes a poisonous type of potato which is still being used by indigenous healers. There are probably just as many recipes with potatoes. One of the most ancient potato dishes is called 'watya' in the Quechua language. This is how the inhabitants of Caral might have cooked the potatoes which they harvested in the fertile Supe River Valley. Without requiring any ceramics or pottery potatoes are simply cooked by covering them with hot rocks and earth ..."

paprika *[pa – 'PREE – ka]*   **"a red powder made
                                                   from sweet peppers"**
*"In the small town of Supe 'paprika' (also called 'pimentón dulce' in
Spanish) is added as a mild condiment to various dishes, including
the 'Tamal Supano'. Usually it is composed of the dried pods of
various sweet peppers which are ground into a fine powder. People
tend to associate 'paprika' with Hungarian cuisine ..."*

pepián *[pe – 'PYAN]*   **"chili sauce; chili stew"**
*"It is also called 'pipián' and is known all over Latin America.
Usually it is thought of as a meat stew. Nowadays, some Peruvian
chefs tend to make this sauce or stew by blending all kinds of chili
peppers with more traditional ingredients such as anchovies. Sauces
and stews were probably unknown to the people of Caral since
ceramics and pottery necessary to prepare dishes like that had not
yet appeared on the Pacific Coast of Peru. A common Quechua word
for 'chili sauce' is 'uchuma'. 'Sauce' (or 'salsa' in Spanish) means
'llaqwa', and 'stew' ('guiso' in Spanish) is known as 'llaqway uchu'
which doubles as a more literal Quechua translation of the word
'pepián'. The Spanish word 'picante' is used for any kind of spicy
stew ..."*

picarones [pee – ka – 'RO – nes]   **"fritters; friedcake"**
"This Peruvian dessert and popular street snack dates back to the colonial era. Usually it comes down to a small fried doughnut often made with pumpkins, brown sugar, cinnamon and maybe some sort of syrup. In the small town of Supe yucca is frequently used which makes it a local delicacy ..."

shicra ['SHEE – kra]   **"woven reed bag"**
"The buildings at the ancient city of Caral are characterized by the so – called 'Shicra' architecture which is typical of the 'Norte Chico' region in Peru. People would weave reeds or grasses into bags which they would fill with rocks. They would then pack the trenches behind the retaining walls of their step pyramids with the stone – filled bags thus building a solid structure that could even resist earthquakes. Architecture was a spiritual practice for the ancient inhabitants of Caral. That way, they built a city with several pyramids, temples and mounds. The word 'shicra' itself seems to mean 'woven reed bag'. But there are no reliable translations of this ancient word. But in Quechua there is a similar word, 'sikra', which means 'woven door'. Other Quechua words for the buildings at Caral include 'pikchu', for 'pyramid', and 'manqos wasi', for 'temple'. The word 'wasi' itself means 'house'. Another important Quechua word is 'waka'. It describes all kinds of temples and shrines built long before the Inca Empire, including those at Caral ..."

tamal *[ta – 'MAL]*   **"tamale"**
"This dish is known all over Latin America. In its most basic form, it consists of cooked corn ground into a paste and mixed with pepper and meat. That mixture is then wrapped in banana leaves and steamed until it is done. It is also a popular snack sold by street vendors. The word 'tamal' itself is derived from Náhuatl, the language which the ancient Olmecs and Aztecs spoke in Mexico. During the colonial era it was introduced in South America. In Quechua the word 'tamal' means 'humint'a' or 'umita' from which the South American Spanish word 'humita' is derived. Generally speaking, it is an alternative form of 'tamal'. However, among indigenous people in the Andes it is known as a sweet snack or dessert wrapped in corn leaves. It is referred to as p'anqas' in the Quechua language ..."

yuca *['YOO – ka]*   **"yucca; manioc; cassava"**
"People use the root of this tropical tree to obtain a starch or flour. Manioc flour is very common in Brazilian cuisine. In Colombia 'yuca' is a popular side dish. In Peru it is used for all kinds of dishes. Originally it comes from the Amazon region (commonly referred to as 'la Selva' in Peru). In the Quechua language it is known as 'rumu'. It is often used as a substitute for potatoes ..."

'Speeches & Specifics ...'

"Saber más es ser más libre." *
César Vallejo, Peruvian poet

* *"More knowledge means more freedom."*

We have just arrived at the ancient city of Caral, Peru. So, let's meet Coral Herencia, a ceremonial leader at the archaeological site ..."

"My name is Coral Herencia.

It is an honor for me to be here on the sacred lands of Caral. And it has been a privilege for me to share the ancient wisdom of our ancestors with people from all over the world. So, last night I have conducted a ceremony called 'Tribute to the Earth Mother'.

It is an ancient form of Thanksgiving in which we human beings connect with Mother Nature. It is a timeless way of giving thanks which we call 'Ayni' (or 'Reciprocity') in Quechua. It consists of giving and of receiving. As part of this ancient ritual we make offerings to the Earth Mother.

We offer Her our best crops and produce. At the same time we pray to the Earth Mother, which we call 'Pachamama' in Quechua. And we ask Her to bless our crops and produce. And the ancient city of Caral allows us to remember that sacred relationship ..."

"Now, who are we going to meet in the Caral / Supe area …"

nombres / names …	activities / actividades …	places / lugares …
"Coral Herencia"	"maestra ceremonial; artesana" "ceremonial leader; artisan"	"zona arqueológica de Caral" "archaeological site of Caral"
"Juan Carlos Albújar Pereyra"	"líder municipal" "municipal leader"	"Parque Infantil, Supe"
"Chapi"	"vendedora" "vendor"	"Mercado, Supe"
"Dino Augurto"	"guía" "guide"	"Plaza, Supe"; "zona arqueológica de Caral" "archaeological site of Caral"
"Ruth Shady Solís"	"arqueóloga" "archaeologist"	"zona arqueológica de Caral" "archaeological site of Caral"

"What is the recipe for your favorite dish ?"

"One of my favorite dishes is 'cuy', or 'guinea pig'. Here, in this area, people mostly prepare roasted guinea pig which they serve with white rice and with red potatoes. Usually there is a Peruvian hot sauce called 'ají' that goes with with it. In this area, the hot sauce is made with paprika. And so, this is one of the most popular dishes in this entire region. 'Arroz con Pato', a 'Duck and Rice Casserole', is another dish which is typical of this area. Basically, it is like a stew. But there are many other dishes. Personally, I think that the most typical food item here is the 'Tamal Supano'.

It is made with ground corn which is mixed with 'ají', chicken or pork meat, and ...

It has a specific reddish color due to the paprika which we put in the 'ají' sauce. We also add a little bit of anise and some peanuts to give it a distinct flavor. And this dough is wrapped in banana leaves. This is what we call a 'tamal'. Then we boil it for two to three hours. And this is how the excellent 'Tamal Supano' is made ..."

- Juan Carlos Albújar Pereyra,
  local leader in the 'Caral – Supe' area ...

"Well ...

For me, as a 'Norteño', as a 'Northerner', it would be a dish from my home region. It would be a 'Seco de Cabrito A La Norteña' (a goat stew from Northern Peru). There are many fish recipes as well. But it's the seasoning that makes all the difference; the way we season our dishes in northern Peru is different from the way people season their dishes in the mountains (the Peruvian Andes) and in the coastal region of Peru. But every region in this country has a typical dish. And its flavor depends on where it is prepared and cooked."

- Dino Augurto,
  interpretive guide at the archaeological site of Caral ...

"Here is a list of the favorite dishes mentioned by some of the locals in the Caral / Supe area …"

dish ...	participant ...	origin ...
"Cuy Frito" "Fried Guinea Pig"	"Juan Carlos Albújar Pereyra"	"Supe region"
"Arroz con Pato" "Duck and Rice Casserole"	"Juan Carlos Albújar Pereyra"	"Northern Peru"
"Tamales Supanos" "Tamales from Supe"	"Juan Carlos Albújar Pereyra"	"Supe region"
"Seco de Cabrito A La Norteña" "Northern Goat Stew"	"Dino Augurto"	"Northern Peru"
"Picarones de Yuca" "Cassava Fritters"	"Chapi"	"Supe region"

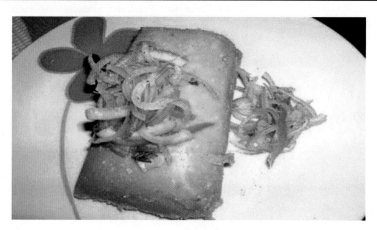

<u>"And how did you learn this recipe ?"</u>

"This is a local recipe.
You know, we are all millionaires here, in Peru.
Everything is available; fresh fish from the sea, as well as potatoes and wheat from the Andes …
Wherever you go in this country you will find a culinary treasure.
Each community has a traditional dish.
And here, in the Supe valley, people grow yucca (or manioc).
That is why we have this little treasure here, the 'Picarones de Yuca'. But there is a lot more you can make with yucca (or cassava), such as cakes and sweets …"

- Chapi,
  market vendor in Supe …

<u>"What do people here drink to accompany or digest a meal ?"</u>

"People in this area usually have wine during or after a meal. It is a dry wine. Maybe they also have a glass of Pisco, Peruvian Pisco. There are some local wines here.
And there are quite a few vineyards in the countryside near Supe. Some of our local wines are known nationwide and in other countries as well. And our wines are being sold both in Peru and in other countries now.
So we have some very good wines in this area."

- Juan Carlos Albújar Pereyra,
  local leader in the 'Caral – Supe' area …

"You could have some tea; chamomile tea, for example, or any other kind of tea …
But this is just a snack which you could eat in your car while you are driving. This is a good snack which could be eaten anytime you feel hungry."

- Chapi,
  market vendor in Supe …

"Here we have a list of drinks and beverages which could be paired with some of the dishes mentioned above …"

bebida / beverage …	participante / participant …	plato / dish …
"un vino seco local" "a local dry wine" "un Pisco"	"Juan Carlos Albújar Pereyra"	"Cuy Frito" "Arroz con Pato" "Tamales Supanos"
"Chicha de Guayaba" "Guava Chicha"	"Dino Augurto"	"Seco de Cabrito A La Norteña"
"una manzanilla" "(Chamomile) Tea"	"Chapi"	"Picarones de Yuca"

"What did people eat here 5,000 years ago ?"

"This is quite an important question and I feel honored to be able to answer it. That's because, on one hand, this is part of our research, and, on the other hand, we keep finding evidence of what people have eaten in Caral 5,000 years ago. As a matter of fact, the ancient people of Caral mixed food scraps with earth. Then they used that mixture as a filling material for the construction of their buildings. And that's why we know that the Pacific Ocean was a key food source for them. Especially anchovies, which are rich in protein, were part of their daily food diet. People also ate other sea fish such as sea bass, albacore tuna, and so on. They ate mollusks such as giant mussels, blue mussels, shellfish and various types of clams. And they raised crops such as beans, squash, melons, pumpkins, and so on. And they ate fruit; two types of the guava fruit were known to them, for example. Something else which I would like to mention is that we have also excavated food items and objects from the Amazon region, from the northern desert and from the Pacific Coast. So, this tells us that these people used to trade with each other thousands of years ago. Here, in Peru, we have a specific word for that sort of trade which is 'trueque', or 'barter'. It consisted of exchanging food items, crafts and commodities along ancient trade routes. The entire economy was based on that mechanism. And here, in Caral and in the Supe valley, agriculture was a predominant economic factor. Another important factor which I would like to mention is that nowadays, when we want to celebrate or just have a drink with friends, we have a beer, a soft drink or some mineral water in this country. But, again, Doctor Shady Solís has found evidence of two types of the guava fruit at the archaeological site of Caral. And we have concluded that the ancient people of Caral probably made and consumed 'chicha de guayaba', a guava beer, or fermented guava chicha, during ceremonies and major events ..."

- Dino Augurto,
  interpretive guide at the archaeological site of Caral ..."

"People would share their native plants and crops with you such as squash or pumpkins. They would make beverages and juices from local fruits and vegetables.
They would even share their medicinal plants and herbs with you. And that is because people were willing to share everything equally back then. People in Caral would also share their astronomical knowledge with you."

- Coral Herencia,
  ceremonial leader at the archaeological site of Caral ..."

"So, here is a shopping list of the food items which people consumed in Caral thousands of years ago and which can still be found and bought at the market in the Caral / Supe region nowadays ..."

producto comestible / food item ...	recomendado por / recommended by ...
"anchoveta, lorna, robalo, bonito, furel, choro zapato, choro azul, macha, almeja, zapallos, frejoles, calabazas, luma, guayaba, pacay ..."	"Dino Augurto"
"anchovy, drum fish, black snook fish, mackerel, giant mussels, blue mussels, razor clams, clams, squash, beans, pumpkins, myrtle, guava, ice – cream beans ..."	
"plantas nativas, zapallos, semillas, agüitas, medicinas ..."	"Coral Herencia"
"native plants, pumpkins, seeds, potions, medicine ..."	

"How has your cultural identity changed since the discovery of Caral ?"

"Well, I would tell you this …
I am the child of a Peruvian mother whereas my father came from another country. My dad came from Czechoslovakia. And he loved and admired this country. But very often he would ask, 'How can Peruvians not be aware of the richness of their cultural heritage ?'
He always took us to all kinds of archaeological sites when I was a child. So, since I was a little girl I dreamed of becoming an archaeologist. Since my early childhood I knew that this would be my destiny. And I had no doubt about which discipline I would choose when I decided to go to college. So, to me, the significance of the Caral Civilization is this …
It is a civilization which should teach us a lesson; it teaches us how to manage our lives as Peruvians. We have to learn how to work together. We have to recognize our problems and find solutions together. We all have to learn how to work together, like a community. We have to stop thinking that the only way to succeed consists of harming others, of being bigger and better than others and of competing with one another. We have to get rid of this concept which I call the 'vision of a crab'.
I don't know if you are all familiar with the story of the crabs …
There were two containers; in one of them there were Peruvian crabs and in the other one there were crabs from other countries. The foreign crabs managed to climb out of the container. Some of them even climbed into the container with the Peruvian crabs to help them to escape. But none of the Peruvian crabs managed to climb out because the other Peruvian crabs would keep holding them back. And this has to change. This is the concept which I am talking about. We have to change our way of thinking. And this is why we have launched a network of community museums, including the one in Supe.

Our goal is to open more community museums in this area. We would like those museums to be places where people would learn about our social history and start thinking about our present condition. We want people to learn from the past in order to improve their own living conditions. This is the lesson we all have to learn. We have to learn how to work together and how to develop this country together ..."

- Ruth Shady Solís,
  archaeologist at the archaeological site of Caral ..."

<u>"What can today's society learn from a culture
that existed 5,000 years ago ?"</u>

"Well, this is an interesting question ...
I believe that one of the missions of an archaeologist is to find out how people managed and subdivided the land in the Andean region. Land management depended on the specific characteristics and physical features of a particular area.
So, the Caral Civilization had a comprehensive notion of land management. Nowadays we follow the model which the Spaniards have introduced in Peru and in South America. It is a European model based on the idea that the land should be subdivided into regions and provinces. But the Native American notion of land management ignored such artificial subdivisions.
Now this country is subdivided into departments. And, again, this is a Spanish legacy. And, as an archaeologist, I am trying to promote the indigenous notion of land management which ignores artificial borders and subdivisions. Recently I have talked with the mayor of Barranca about this; and I have told him that Peru should create a 'Commonwealth of provinces and regions'. The idea is to form a community that takes into account the physical features of the land and the needs of the population. Such a wide – ranging notion of subdividing the land could reach from the Pacific Coast across the Andes all the way to the Amazon Basin. That way, sometime in the future, land management would be based on people's needs.
Maybe this would allow people in rural areas to have better opportunities so that they wouldn't have to go to the major urban centers, become illegal land squatters living in shantytowns and slums on the outskirts of town.
So, my hope is that one day, as a country, Peru will be managed and subdivided more harmoniously than it is now."

- Ruth Shady Solís,
  archaeologist at the archaeological site of Caral ..."

"I am afraid that people wouldn't understand us.
Our ancestors would think that we have lost our minds. There is no more respect in the world. Families are falling apart. People no longer take care of the environment. But our grandfathers had a vision. They said that 500 years after the Spanish Conquest there would be a second Renaissance; an indigenous Renaissance.
And you know why ?
Life occurs in cycles, one cycle after another. And now the second Renaissance has arrived.
That's why we are here. That's why I am standing here, as a 'maestra' (a spiritual leader), in my traditional outfit, remembering that I am a child of the earth. That's why I keep singing the ancient songs in my indigenous language. Those songs contain timeless secrets. I mean, our ancestors, the ancient inhabitants of Caral, would pull our ears if they saw us.
They would ask us, 'Why have you forgotten ?'
Our grandfathers have told us that we, their grandchildren, are the dreams of our ancestors. They left us this legacy, those buildings and those structures, so that we would never forget who we are and where we are coming from. And so, here we are."

- Coral Herencia,
  ceremonial leader at the archaeological site of Caral …"

'Synthesis ...'

...

'The act of 'Blind Tasting' can be associated with the practice of 'sampling and savoring' all sorts of meals, drinks, music, attractions and activities without really knowing too much about them. So, this guidebook is meant to allow a reader or traveler to get a cultural experience just like that. The idea is to help you 'get lost out there'. If something like that happened, you might want to be able to speak with the locals, enjoy their food, listen to their music and appreciate their arts. And once you are able to do just that you might spontaneously want to raise your arms and exclaim, 'I am happy !'

And this deep and profound experience of 'cultural immersion' might even enrich your journey. Eventually, you would even 'find your way around'.

'Beyond Time' is a unique guidebook and documentary based on the interviews with 5 'locals & protagonists' from the Caral / Supe area. Their testimonies about their home region are compiled in this guidebook and the corresponding documentary.

Through their voices the readers, or audience, are supposed to get a genuine perspective of the place. Their experiences provide an intriguing angle to all sorts of sites, attractions and activities.

By the way, this material is also a source for teaching Spanish and Hispanic Culture and Civilization to a French – speaking and English – speaking audience, especially children, with the support of local schools and institutions ...

Situations & Snapshots ...

'Situations' are composed of the personal experiences of the author, or authors. It is a compilation of stories and anecdotes which the reader or traveler might experience on his or her own journey. It includes a section entitled 'Locals & Protagonists' in which several characters encountered and interviewed by the author, or authors, are listed as additional destinations and attractions. 'Snapshots' refer to the pictures taken or compiled in a given area. They are derived from and related to the stories and anecdotes and are meant to enhance them visually with captions taken from the original text. Altogether, 'Situations & Snapshots' combine the portraits of the participants with the author's, or authors', personal experiences and observations and are weaved into a narrative.
So, this chapter goes hand in hand with the interviews and the corresponding documentary which this guidebook is based on ...

Sites & Sensations ...

Here, so – called 'logistical information' is blended with 'Chef's recommendations' about the preparation of some of the local dishes and with (mostly musical) excerpts from songs that are inspired by the place which you get to know. 'Sites' refer to the 'logistical' part, and they stick to the places where the author, or authors, have actually been and which any reader or traveler might enjoy. They include 'websites' and 'contacts' which allow the virtual reader or traveler to find more information on the internet. 'Sensations' describe the dishes, songs, attractions and activities which make you want to forget the tangible information which has just been mentioned. Some of the entries include quotes and testimonies taken from the interviews with the 'locals & protagonists'.
Additional information collected by the author, or authors, who even cooked and documented some of the meals described in this section at different places in the world using respectively local ingredients is also included here. This is precisely what the virtual reader or traveler might want to do at home.
In other words, this chapter is a way of sharing practical and logistical information that you could find in any guidebook with the audience. But here, the information is based on the author's, or authors', personal experiences at those places and on the testimonies provided by the locals who have been interviewed as part of this project. It is also a way of sharing the simple pleasures, tastes, smells and sounds of the area you might want to visit, with a particular emphasis on recipes and other culinary experiences, on the music and lyrics that illustrate the place, and, again, on people's testimonies and comments ...

Sketches & Statistics ...

This section simply boils down to some cultural and historical facts, data and figures combined with maps and illustrations. 'Statistics' refer to the former and tend to be organized in a chronological way. 'Sketches' are composed of the latter and are deliberately distributed among the cold numbers.

This is the outcome of a long, and often tedious process of researching. In other words, you will see the results of a little bit of a treasure hunt for numbers and figures that are both random and intriguing. It's a peculiar way to look at miscellaneous facts interspersed with cartoons, drawings, maps and other forms of visual illustration, including the occasional plain picture ...

Sounds & Symbols ...

Following the tradition of an encyclopedia dating back to the Enlightenment, this glossary provides an insight into the linguistic and cultural background of a place. Like any encyclopedia it is meant to inform without pretending to be complete. It should arouse curiosity and motivate any potential reader to become a traveler and explore the place mentioned in this cultural guidebook. Some of the most relevant local or indigenous words and expressions representative of the cultural practices in a given area are also included whenever possible. In 'Sounds' a simple form of phonetic transcription is used to give the reader or traveler an idea of what a place might sound like. 'Symbols' is the result of a personal selection process by the author, or authors, and compile the most significant items, objects, names and icons which represent the place described in this cultural guidebook. All the entries are classified in an alphabetical order and selected according to their importance as 'symbols', or emblems, of the place you might want to visit. And then, again, there is the notion of what your potential destination 'sounds' like. A book like this usually describes what you are going to see and experience through words and pictures. But wouldn't you want to hear the place through its accents, dialects, languages, music and even phonetic transcriptions ...

Speeches & Specifics ...

In this chapter you hear the voices of locals and protagonists of all walks of life. They become your personal guides and teachers. Excerpts and quotes from interviews conducted by the author, or authors, allow you to experience a place from their perspective and to look at it through their eyes. These testimonies should give you a deeper insight into the local culture and even help you to learn, understand and speak a little bit of the local or indigenous language or dialect. In that respect, people become destinations not to be missed. In 'Speeches', you find the testimonies of the 'locals & protagonists' talking about their hometown and the surrounding region.
'Specifics' mostly consist of a list of recommendations and experiences which people are willing to share with travelers and visitors.
The whole chapter serves as an introduction into the local language or dialect and is meant to give you an idea of how people really speak in the area you are about to discover. So, again, in 'Speeches & Specifics', we can hear and read people's testimonies directly. Sometimes there is only one answer; sometimes there are several answers to a specific question asked by the author, or authors. And then a list with excerpts and quotes taken from the comments and statements made by other locals, often with some insight into the local accent and language, completes the information ...

the author ...

Marco Rixecker is the creator and author of the 'Blind Taste Cultural Guidebooks' series. They are derived from interviews conducted with 'locals & protagonists' and from his personal observations and travel notes. For years he has traveled on historic roads and itineraries such as 'Route 66', the 'Lewis & Clark Trail' and the 'Pan – American Highway'. He is a freelance journalist, reporter, cook, writer, poet, singer and songwriter, and speaks several languages. And he keeps traveling the world.

This cultural guidebook has been written with the Peruvian journalist Luis Deza León. He can conduct and organize daytrips and overnight excursions to Caral and to the Supe River Valley out of his hometown, Lima.

Marco can organize these and other cultural expeditions hand in hand with language lessons, cooking classes and other services ...

Email (Marco Rixecker & Luis Deza León).:
contact.aulamundi@gmail.com

Northern Peru has often been described as the Egypt of South America. Between Ecuador and Lima countless archaeological sites, ancient cities and unexplored ruins await the traveler willing to deviate from the Pan – American Highway and to see more of Peru than Cuzco or Machu Picchu. Near the capital, Lima, there is a small town by the name of Supe.

From there, a side road goes to the ancient city of Caral. It is thought to be the oldest city in the Americas and one of the oldest developed settlements in the world.

There is Egypt. There is Mesopotamia.
And there is Caral, in Peru,
which is more than 5,000 years old ...

"And the story goes on from there ... "

Victor Reece, Tsimpsian storyteller,
First Nations, Canada

***

You might also be interested in …

"Speeches & Specifics (Discursos & Detalles) # 1:
A five - step introduction into Peruvian Spanish"

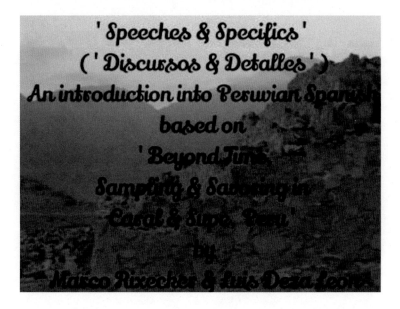

It's a complete Spanish course based on this guidebook.

Please go to:

www.amazon.com

***

Made in United States
Orlando, FL
11 October 2023

37798764R00058